THE LASER BOOK

Corrected for the 1997–2000 Rules of Sailing

THE LASER BOOK

Tim Davison

photographs by Tim Hore

© Fernhurst Books 1992

First edition published 1979
Second edition published 1987

Third edition published 1992 by Fernhurst Books,
Duke's Path, High Street, Arundel, West Sussex, BN18 9AJ, England

All rights reserved. No part of this publication may be reproduced,
stored in a retrieval system, or transmitted in any form or by any
means, electronic, mechanical, photocopying, recording or
otherwise, without the prior permission of Fernhurst Books.

British Library Cataloguing in Publication Data

Davison, Tim
Laser Book. – 3Rev.ed
I.Title
623.88223

ISBN 0-906754 78 X

Printed and bound in Great Britain

Acknowledgements
The publishers would like to thank David Johnson for his input
to the third edition, and for helming in the new photographs
which were taken at Oxford Sailing Club. David Hitchcock and Tim
Davison helmed in the photo sessions held at the Queen Mary
Sailing Club, Ashford, Middlesex.
    The author is very grateful to the following people for their
helpful comments on the manuscript: Nigel Vick, Geoff Crowther,
Nick Livingstone, Richard Simmons, Ian Clayton of the National
Sailing Centre, Cowes, and Anthea Thomson.

The following photographs are reproduced by kind permission
of the International Laser Class Association: pages 2-3, 32, 39,
40, 43, 49, 51 (bottom), 56, 64. All other photographs by Tim
Hore and John Woodward.

The cover photograph is courtesy of Geoff Martin of I.L.C.A. The
cover design is by Behram Kapadia.

Design: John Woodward
Artwork: PanTek, Maidstone
Composition: A&G Phototypesetters, Knaphill, plus CST Eastbourne
Printed by Hillman Printers, Frome

Contents

1 Introduction

Welcome to *The Laser Book*!

Whether you're a complete beginner or a club racer, this manual was written to help you get into top gear. I've tried hard to answer the key questions while keeping the book logical and lively. And I have tried out the ideas, both on the race course and when coaching. They do work!

The photographs are a major feature of the book. They were taken by Tim Hore and John Woodward at Queen Mary Sailing Club and at Oxford Sailing Club, and are a tribute to their skill.

Chapter 16, Looking after your Laser, was kindly provided by John Heath.

Finally, my thanks to Peter Smith and the UK Laser Association. The idea was theirs, and without their help and cheerful criticism there would have been no book.

This third edition is right up-to-date, especially in terms of sailing technique, rig controls and their adjustment. Now, as they say, it's up to the nut on the end of the tiller.

Good sailing!

Tim Davison

The Laser is beautifully simple. It has the minimum number of parts, each carefully designed to do a specific job. However, there are a few things you can do ashore to make life easier when you go afloat.

The painter
Tie a six-metre length of rope to the plastic eye near the bow. This is long enough for mooring and for towing the boat. Tie the loose end round the mast when sailing.

The centreboard
If you capsize and the boat turns upside down, the centreboard may fall out. To prevent this, pass a length of shockcord through the centreboard, through the plastic eye near the bow and back the other side of the mast. The two ends are held together with C-clips. Tension sufficiently to hold the board firm.

Drill two holes near the top of the board and fit a rope handle. This makes it much easier to raise.

The rudder
The rudder can also fall out if the boat turns upside down. It does *not* float, so make sure the rudderstop holds it in place. If not, loosen the screws and adjust it.

Tape the mainsheet and traveller blocks to prevent kinking. Cover the tiller with a piece of washing-up liquid bottle to prevent wear. Tie the traveller with a small knot, as far aft as possible.

Tighten the bolt through the rudder head. If there is any slack the cheeks of the head may buckle when you turn. You should be able to raise the blade – it will then stay up while you launch the boat.

Shockcord and a handle attached to the centreboard.

Adjust the rudderstop so it holds the rudder in place.

There should be no gap between the rudderstop and pintle.

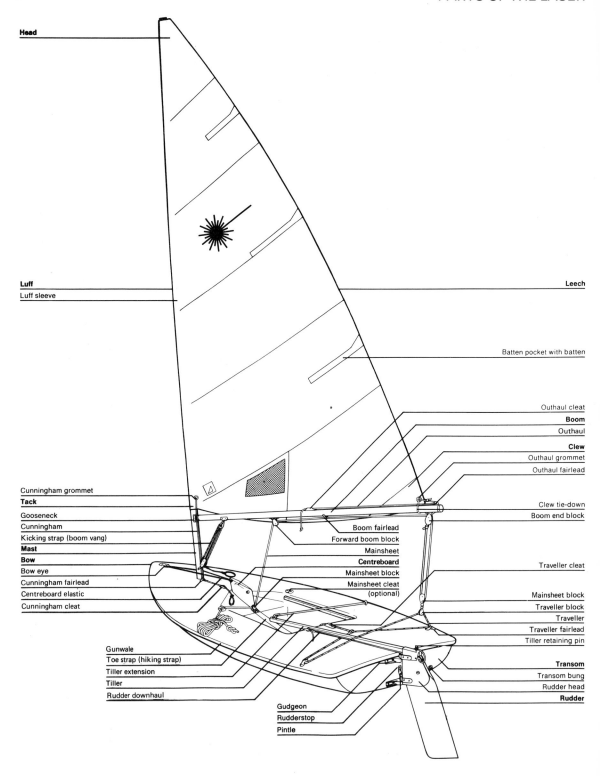

Head

Luff
Luff sleeve

Leech

Batten pocket with batten

Outhaul cleat
Boom
Outhaul
Clew
Outhaul grommet
Outhaul fairlead

Cunningham grommet
Tack
Clew tie-down
Gooseneck
Boom end block
Cunningham
Kicking strap (boom vang)
Boom fairlead
Mast
Forward boom block
Bow
Mainsheet
Bow eye
Centreboard
Traveller cleat
Cunningham fairlead
Mainsheet block
Centreboard elastic
Mainsheet cleat
Mainsheet block
Cunningham cleat
(optional)
Traveller block
Traveller
Traveller fairlead
Tiller retaining pin

Gunwale
Toe strap (hiking strap)
Transom
Tiller extension
Transom bung
Tiller
Rudder head
Rudder downhaul
Rudder

Gudgeon
Rudderstop
Pintle

The tiller

This corresponds to the steering wheel of your car – no slack is expected! If the fit of the tiller in the rudder head is poor, take the tiller out and squeeze the sides of the head in a vice until the slack disappears.

You may like to shorten the tiller so it does not project into the cockpit – this makes steering easier when you're sitting back on a broad reach or run.

Don't use the retaining pin in the stock – the mainsheet just catches on it.

The tiller extension

The metal tiller extension is quite slippery, so stick some tape round it every few centimetres. This makes a series of ridges which stop your hand sliding. You may find you need to fit a longer tiller extension; you must be able to steer easily when hiking at full stretch or when sitting forward of the centreboard in light airs.

Toe strap (hiking strap)

The photos show how to rig a rope so you can adjust the toe strap while sailing. Experiment until the loosest setting is right for beating (top photo) and the tightest is spot on for reaching (bottom photo). When hiking, your thighs should be on the outside edge of the deck.

Fit an elastic loop through the back loop of the toe strap and around the traveller cleat. This keeps the toe strap tight when not in use and makes it easier to hook your feet under it.

The toe strap elastic and adjusting rope.

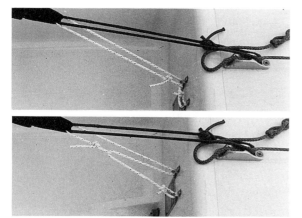

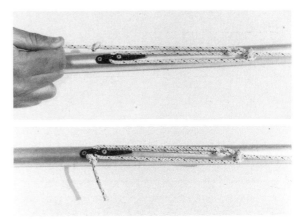

Tie the rudder downhaul like this: the knot will pull off the cleat if the blade runs aground.

Self bailer

The Laser is not supplied with a self bailer, but one can easily be added. It gets rid of water more quickly than the bailing hole; the only thing to remember is to push it up when coming ashore, or it will be broken on the beach.

Gooseneck

The gooseneck bolt needs tightening after every few outings. Tighten it as much as possible – this helps prevent the gooseneck bending and stops the boom wobbling.

Burgee (flag)

The burgee must be balanced properly, or it will give misleading information when the boat heels. To balance a burgee, hold it with the stick horizontal: if the flag itself flops downwards, wind tape round the balance wire to give it more weight. When it is balanced, the burgee will stay level when you pick it up.

Put tape around the middle and bottom of the burgee stick. When you push it into the sail sleeve at the front or back of the mast, the tape will stop the burgee sliding around.

Side cleats for the mainsheet

These should only be used when you need a free hand for something else. At other times the centre ratchet block will take most of the mainsheet's load particularly if you have the kicking strap (vang) tight. You may even decide to take off the side cleats, as many sailors do.

3 Rigging

Once you're used to it, the Laser can be rigged in under ten minutes. A sensible order for putting it together is given below: the boat should then look like the diagram on page 8.

1 Put on the traveller with the mainsheet and traveller blocks. Don't forget the bung!

2 Rig the rest of the mainsheet.

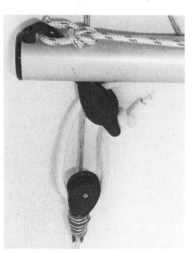

3 Tie the outhaul rope to the fairlead at the end of the boom using a bowline knot.

4 Fix the kicking strap (vang) to the mast. Note the swivel. The 8:1 purchase and handle are all one piece of rope.

5 Fit the masts together.

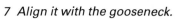

6 *Slide the sail onto the mast.*

7 *Align it with the gooseneck.*

8 *Put in the burgee, at the front or back of the mast.*

9 *Put in the battens: centre the inboard end on the elastic . . .*

10 *. . . then slide the outboard end across so it is held.*

11 *Wipe any dirt off the foot of the mast and check there is none in the mast hole. Check there are no electric cables overhead.*

12 *Fit the mast into the boat. If it is windy point the mast into the wind, which will support it as you guide the foot into the hole.*

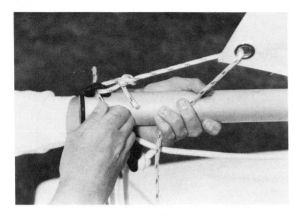

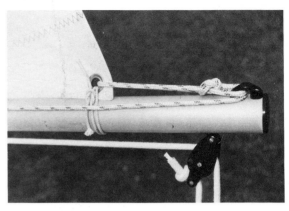

13 Take the boat to the water's edge. Push the boom into the gooseneck. Then rig the outhaul rope.

14 Tie a length of pre-stretched rope through the clew and around the boom, inside the outhaul. Without this the boom will hang down and you cannot sheet in hard on the beat.

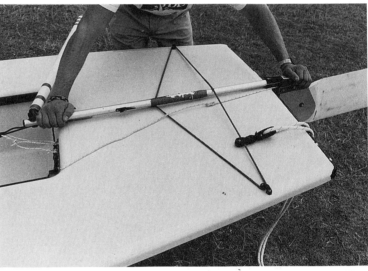

15 Set up the kicking strap (vang) and rig the cunningham rope like this (see page 13 for details).

16 Put on the rudder and tiller, making sure that the tiller goes under the traveller. Check that it clears the traveller knot. Put the centreboard into the boat and you're ready to go sailing.

Reefing

If the wind is strong, you can reduce sail by reefing. Take out the top batten, and put the mast and sail into the mast hole. Push the cunningham rope through the sail. Keeping the rope tight, twist the mast. When you have enough rolls (three, four or five), finish rigging the cunningham, keeping it tight to stop the rolls unwinding. Make sure the rope lashing the sail clew to the boom is tight, or the boom will flop down into the boat.

Tie the outhaul rope directly to the sail. Set up the kicking strap (vang) – use only enough tension to keep the boom horizontal.

4 Sail controls

Apart from the mainsheet and the traveller, three ropes control the shape of the sail. These are the cunningham, the outhaul and the kicking strap (vang).

The sail is cut so that it sets with a curve, or belly. The larger the curve, the more drive the sail has, but the larger the heeling effect. Adjusting the sail controls alters the curve in the sail. The curve should be larger for reaching and running, smaller for beating and in strong winds.

The kicking strap (vang) pulls down on the boom. This stops the sail twisting, and also bends the mast, flattening the sail. The cunningham and outhaul also flatten the sail when pulled tight.

Cunningham

There are many ways of rigging the cunningham. A simple method giving a 4:1 purchase is shown. Use thin line so the system goes slack when uncleated. Note the ropes all go past the same side of the boom, so the cringle can be pulled right down to the gooseneck when beating in a blow.

But to begin with, tighten the cunningham as much as you can with one hand and leave it set like this while sailing.

1 Tie a bowline as shown.

2 Tie the middle of the rope around the vang swivel.

3 Rig the other end through the bowline.

4 Pass it through the fairlead and cleat, and make a handle.

Outhaul

A simple method of rigging the outhaul is shown on the right. This gives a 2:1 purchase.

The outhaul controls the curve in the bottom part of the sail. If it is tight, the sail is flat. If it is loose, a powerful curve forms.

If you are a beginner, you don't need to adjust the outhaul while sailing. A more experienced sailor will tighten it when beating, and loosen it when reaching and running. In strong winds, have the outhaul tighter than in light winds. A loose setting will result in a gap of about 20cm between the middle of the boom and the foot of the sail; in very strong winds, the setting should be tight enough for the foot to just touch the boom with wind in the sail.

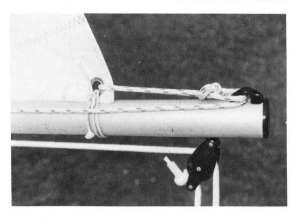

Above: Tie the rope to the boom fitting, lead it through the eye and back through the fitting.

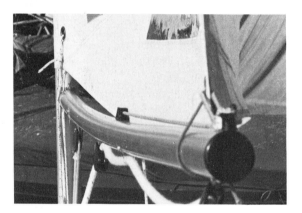

Above: With the outhaul loose, there is a 20cm gap between the boom and the foot of the sail.

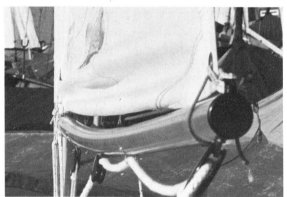

Above: with a tight outhaul, the foot will just touch the boom with no wind in the sail.

To tighten the outhaul on the beat, cleat the main and pull the outhaul sideways.

Then tension the tail by sliding the knot towards the mast.

Kicking strap (vang)

The kicking strap controls the twist in the back of the sail. It also controls mast bend, and hence the curve of the sail.

A simple way of setting the kicking strap is to tighten the traveller, pull in the mainsheet fully and cleat it. Grab the handle on the kicking strap. Put one foot on the mainsheet, between the forward boom block and the ratchet block. Push hard with your foot, at the same time pulling the kicking strap tight. Finally cleat off the kicking strap. You may now need to let out the mainsheet a bit to help you pick up speed.

Paint three marks on the kicking strap rope to give a visual indication of its tightness. Set up the boat on land and pull in the mainsheet until the back blocks touch. Paint the marks in line across the three parts of the purchase to indicate 'normal' kicking strap tension. If you are a beginner, you can leave the kicking strap in this position while sailing.

In strong winds the kicking strap must be a lot tighter (super-vanging) while in light winds it can be a little looser than the 'normal' setting.

To slacken the rope get a good grip and jerk it out of the cleat. It's a good idea to tie a knot in the line to stop it running out too far.

The kicking strap gives the sail power. When you come ashore loosen it as soon as you can to quieten the boat down.

If the kicking strap is too loose the boom will lift, putting too much twist in the sail.

To tighten the kicking strap, pull in the mainsheet and cleat it.

Grab the kicking strap and pull it tight while pushing down on the mainsheet with your foot.

Cleat the kicking strap, hike and go!

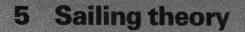

5 Sailing theory

Take a careful look at this photograph. You will see that:

- The helmsman always sits on the windward side of the boat (to balance the wind pushing on the sail).
- The helmsman always holds the tiller in his aft (back) hand. He steers with the tiller.
- The helmsman always holds the mainsheet in his forward (front) hand. The mainsheet adjusts the angle of the sail to the centreline of the boat.

How does the boat sail?

Wind is the boat's driving force. The wind flows over the windward side of the sail (causing pressure) and round the leeward side (causing suction). The resulting force on the sail is in the direction of arrow A, at right angles to the sail.

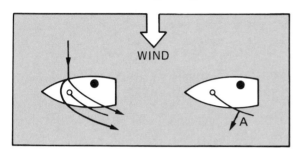

The force pushes the boat forwards and sideways. The forward push is welcome! The sideways push is counteracted by water pressure on the centreboard.

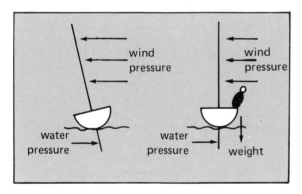

The helmsman's weight counteracts the turning (capsizing) effect. The further he leans out, the more leverage he gets.

If the sail is pulled in, force A will be almost at right angles to the boat: the sideways force is maximum, and the centreboard needs to be

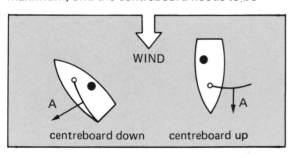

centreboard down   centreboard up

pushed right down. If the sail is let out, force A points forwards: there is no sideways force, so the centreboard can be pulled up.

How can I steer?

When a boat is sailing straight, the water flows past the rudder undisturbed. When the rudder is turned, the water is deflected. The water hitting the rudder pushes it, and the back of boat, in direction B. The bow turns to the left.

In short, pulling the tiller towards you turns the bow away from you, and vice versa.

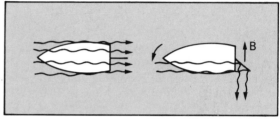

How can I stop?

It is the wind in the sail that makes a boat go forward. To stop it, take the wind out of the sail either by letting go of the mainsheet, or by altering course towards the wind.

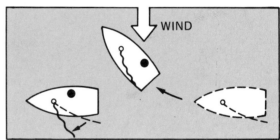

How can I tell which way the wind is blowing?

Everything in sailing is related to the wind direction. You can tell which way it's blowing by the feel of it on your cheek, by the wave direction or by using a burgee. Remember, the burgee points to where the wind is going.

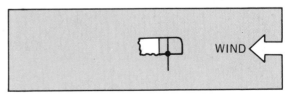

Points of sailing

Look at the diagram on the opposite page. There are three points of sailing:

- *Reaching* – the boat sails *across* the wind.
- *Beating* – the boat sail *towards* the wind.
- *Running* – the boat sails with the wind *behind* it.

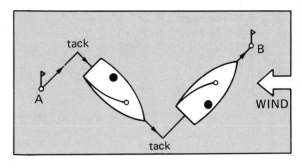

Reaching

When reaching, the boat sails at right angles to the wind, which is blowing from behind your back. The sail should be about halfway out and the centreboard halfway up.

Beating

If you want to change course towards the wind, you must push the centreboard down and pull in the sail as you turn. You can go on turning towards the wind until the sail is pulled right in. Then you are *beating*.

If you try to turn further towards the wind you enter the 'no-go area'. The sail flaps and the boat stops.

If you want to reach a point that is upwind of your current position you have to *beat* zigzag fashion, as shown in the diagram.

At the end of each 'zig' the boat turns through an angle of 90°. This is called a *tack*. The boat turns 'through' the wind – the sail blows across to the other side and the helmsman must shift his weight across the boat to balance it.

Running

From a reach, you may want to change course away from the wind. Pull up the centreboard (not more than three-quarters up) and let out the sail as you turn. You can go on turning until the wind is coming from behind the boat. The you are *running*.

If you turn more, the boat will *gybe*. The wind blows from the other side of the boat. You must shift your weight across to balance it.

Reaching.

Beating.

Running.

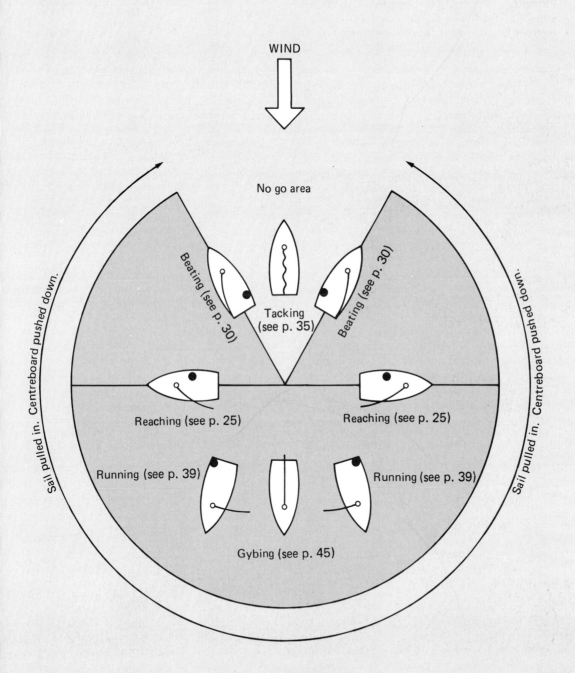

WIND

No go area

Beating (see p. 30)

Tacking (see p. 35)

Beating (see p. 30)

Reaching (see p. 25)

Reaching (see p. 25)

Running (see p. 39)

Running (see p. 39)

Gybing (see p. 45)

Sail pulled in. Centreboard pushed down.

Sail pulled in. Centreboard pushed down.

6 A first sail

Try to choose a day with a gentle breeze for your first sail. Wind is measured either on the Beaufort scale or in metres per second. Force 4 or above would be unsuitable.

A reservoir, river or estuary is a good place to learn to sail. If there is a sailing school that specialises in Laser beginners' courses that's even better. If you are learning on the open sea try to avoid an offshore wind (wind blowing from shore to sea) – you may get blown a long way from the shore. *Always* wear a buoyancy aid or lifejacket, and always stay with the boat.

Rig the boat as described on pages 10-12. Reef if it's very windy. Get a friend to help you launch. He should hold the boat for you while you lower the rudder and put in the centreboard. One good push and you're under way. (Launching is discussed on pages 23-24.)

As soon as you can, get sailing on a reach with the wind blowing at right angles to the boat. The centreboard will be about half up and the sail about half out. Sit on the side opposite the sail. Practise adjusting the mainsheet and steering. Try to get the 'feel' of the boat, particularly using your weight to balance the wind in the sail. (Reaching is discussed on pages 25-29.)

Eventually you will need to tack and reach back again. Try to tack smoothly, changing sides and swapping hands on the tiller and mainsheet as you do so. If the boat stops during a tack, keep the tiller central and wait until the boat starts to drift backwards. Eventually it will turn to one side and you'll be able to get sailing again. (Tacking is discussed on pages 35-38.)

Reach back and forth until you have confidence. Try picking an object and sailing straight towards it, adjusting the mainsheet so the sail is as far out as possible without flapping. If a gust comes, let the mainsheet out.

Next try picking objects slightly closer to or slightly further away from the wind. Try sailing towards them adjusting the mainsheet.

Get sailing on a reach . . .   *Tack round . . .*   *Then reach back.*

Beaufort scale of wind force

Beaufort No.	General Description	At sea	On land	Limits of velocity (metres per second)
0	Calm	Sea like a mirror	Calm; smoke rises vertically	0.5
1	Light Air	Ripples	Direction of wind shown by smoke drift but not by wind vanes.	0.6 – 1.9
2	Light breeze	Small wavelets.	Wind felt on face; leaves rustle.	2.0 – 3.5
3	Gentle breeze	Large wavelets. Crests begin to break.	Leaves and small twigs in constant motion. Wind extends light flags.	3.6 – 5.9
4	Moderate	Small waves becoming longer, fairly frequent white horses.	Raises dust and loose paper; small branches are moved.	6.0 – 9.4
5	Fresh breeze	Moderate waves, many white horses, chance of some spray.	Small tress in leaf begin to sway.	9.5 – 12.4
6	Strong breeze	Large waves begin to form; the white foam crests are more extensive everywhere. Probably some spray.	Large branches in motion Umbrellas used with difficulty.	12.5 – 15.9
7	Near gale	Sea heaps up and white foam from breaking waves begins to be blown in streaks.	Whole trees in motion	16.0 – 19.5

When you've had enough, head for the shore. If the wind is onshore, unhook the mainsheet and traveller blocks when you are about 20 metres away and drift ashore. (If your blocks are fixed together, undo the knot in the mainsheet by the boom end block.) If the wind is offshore, simply sail up to the shore, letting go of the mainsheet as you get near. Don't forget to pull up the rudder and centreboard in good time. (Landing is discussed in more detail on pages 52-53.)

The next steps

When you feel happy reaching and tacking you are ready to try the other points of sailing. You should still reef if it is windy (more than force 2).

One good way to practise is to sail round a square 'course'. From your reach, gradually turn away from the wind, letting out the sail and pulling the centreboard three-quarters up. You are now running. After a while, pull the tiller towards you and gybe. Now reach the other way, with the centreboard half down and the mainsheet half out. Next, push the centreboard right down and turn towards the wind, pulling in your sail. You are beating. Tack, and beat the other way. When you are far enough into the wind, turn off on to a reach, letting the sail out and pulling the centreboard half up. Try sailing several laps.

Remember:
- Sit on the windward side.
- Keep the mainsheet in your front hand, tiller in your back hand.
- If you get out of control, let go of the mainsheet.

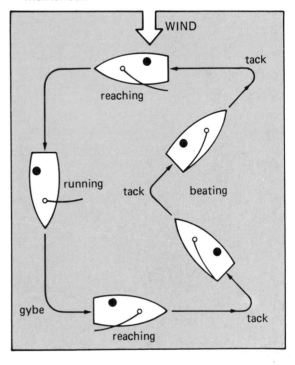

Handling the mainsheet and tiller

When you're sailing you need to adjust the mainsheet and tiller constantly. This is hard to do if the tiller extension is behind you. A better method is to hold it across your body in a 'javelin grip'. Then you can use your tiller extension hand to hold the sheet when, for example, you want to adjust the centreboard. You can also use both hands when winding in the mainsheet and when letting it out.

On a reach take the mainsheet straight from the boom for extra control. Once again, you can use your tiller extension hand to help adjust the mainsheet, or to hold it when you need to take the rope from the mainsheet block once again.

The 'javelin grip'.

Above: Use your tiller hand to trap the mainsheet.

Above: Haul in the sheet with your other hand.

Above: Trap it again to free your mainsheet hand.

Take the mainsheet straight from the boom on a reach: this gives you more control.

To change over trap it with your tiller hand as you take up the slack through the block.

Haul the mainsheet back through the block, using your tiller hand to trap it as before.

7 Launching

With practice, you will find you can get afloat quickly and easily in most conditions.

How you launch depends on the wind direction relative to the shore. However, a few points always apply:

- Rig the boat on the shore.

- Keep the boat pointing into the wind at all times. Let the sail flap freely – make sure the mainsheet is slack.

- If you are not launching immediately and the boat is misbehaving, let off the kicking strap (vang).

- The hull is very easily damaged. Keep it off the ground at all costs.

Launching with the wind along the shore
This is the easiest wind direction to launch in.

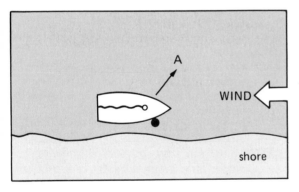

1 Get your boat rigged, but leave the rudder blade up and don't put the centreboard into its slot yet.

2 Put the boat in the water, keeping it pointing into the wind. Stand on the windward side, as near the bow as you can – remember that the boat will pivot about you.

3 See that your trolley is left safely – remember the tide! If you are on a sandy shore, you can leave the boat aground while you move your trolley; if it is rocky, you will need help.

4 Put in the centreboard and push down the rudder until they both just clear the bottom.

5 Make sure your mainsheet is running free and the tiller extension points towards you.

6 Turn the boat slightly away from the shore, push it forward and step in on the windward side. Pull in the sail, encouraging the boat to move forward slowly, and away from, the shore (direction A on the diagram). *Don't* try to go too fast with the rudder blade up – you may bend the rudder head.

7 As soon as the water is deep enough, let out the sail (keeping the boat in direction A) and push the centreboard and rudder right down.

Launching with an offshore wind
Follow *exactly* the same method as for launching with the wind along the shore. DO NOT try to turn the boat round and sail straight out – it will sail away before you have time to jump in! Aim to get off in direction B on the diagram.

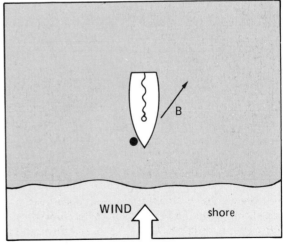

Launching with an onshore wind
This is the most difficult wind direction for launching, because the wind tends to push you back on shore.

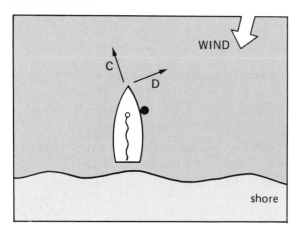

Launch the boat with the mainsheet undone. Then turn the boat head to wind and rig the mainsheet. You will have to beat to get away from the shore, so choose which tack you are going to take. In the diagram, C is better than D because the wind is coming more from the right and C will take you offshore faster.

Give the boat a good push and step aboard. Pull in the sail quickly and hike out. Gradually push the centreboard down as you 'crab' offshore. Finally, when you're well out, stop and lower the rudder blade fully.

Launching in very shallow water
Wade out, towing the boat, until the water is at least up to your knees (deeper if the wind is onshore). Then carry on as described above, according to wind direction.

Launching in waves: onshore wind
Rig the boat at the water's edge with the bow into the wind. Decide which tack you're going off on, and stand on the side that will be to windward. Get the tiller extension out to this side.

Slide the boat into the water, so you're up to your knees. Push down the centreboard as far as you can. Hold the mainsheet in your front hand, and watch for a lull in the waves – it *will* come, but you may have to wait a few minutes. Run forward with the boat, and as it gets deep push the boat forward and haul yourself on board. Hike out, and try to sail as fast as possible. If the boat gets washed back in, jump out to *windward* at the last moment. Try not to get between the boat and the shore – a big wave may push the boat into you and do you a lot of damage. If you do get trapped like this, keep your back to the boat or it may hit your knees 'wrong way on' and break your leg. But if it's that rough, maybe you should stay ashore!

Launching from a jetty
Be sure to launch your boat on the leeward side of the jetty!

To get on the boat, step on to the *middle* of the foredeck and grab the mast. Tip the boat to one side then nimbly slip round the mast on the other side and step into the cockpit.

Push down the rudder and centreboard. Walk along the deck, tipping the boat as described above, and untie the boat. Give a gentle push backwards, retreat to the cockpit, reverse the tiller, pull in the mainsheet and sail off.

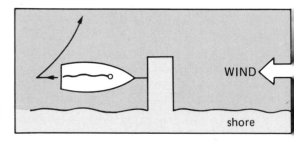

8 Reaching

Reaching is fun! It's the fastest point of sailing and the easiest to control.

What is reaching?
The boats in the diagram below are reaching. Their courses are roughly at right angles to the wind.

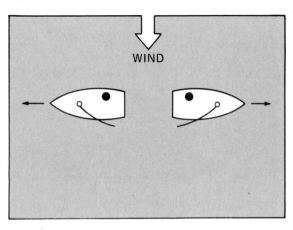

WIND

Adjusting the sail
The secret of reaching is sail trim. Keeping a straight course, let the sail out until the front begins to flap (just behind the mast). Then pull in the sail until it just stops flapping.

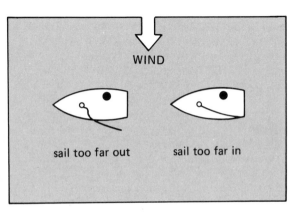

WIND

sail too far out   sail too far in

The wind changes in direction every few seconds, so the sail must be trimmed constantly. Keep the mainsheet in your hand all the time, and 'play' it in and out.

If the sail flaps, it's too far out. If the boat heels over and slows down, the sail is too far in. When the sail is about right, it will be roughly in line with the burgee.

Every time you change course, you must adjust the mainsheet – pull it in further if you change course closer to the wind, let it out if you change course away from the wind.

Steering
Try to keep a reasonably straight course: each time you alter course, you will have to adjust the sail. If there is a strong 'pull' on the tiller extension, it's usually because the boat is heeling over too much. Hike out to bring the boat level; the pull will disappear and you can steer easily.

Trim
Both fore-and-aft and sideways movements of your body affect the boat's trim.

Normally, sit at the front of the cockpit. This presents the best hull shape to the water. Move forwards in light winds to reduce the amount of hull skin in the water (and so reduce skin friction). Move aft in strong winds to lift the bow and help the boat to plane.

Sit on the windward deck and use your weight to keep the boat absolutely upright. This will make steering much easier – if the boat heels, the hull shape becomes asymmetrical and forces the boat to turn to one side.

Centreboard
Keep the centrboard half up, to reduce drag and make the boat easier to handle. If it slips down, tighten the elastic shockcord. If you want to change course closer to the wind, push the centreboard down slightly; pull it up if you change course away from the wind.

Gusts

Look over your shoulder occasionally to see if a gust is coming. The water looks dark as a gust travels over it.

When the gust hits, hike out further. If the boat still heels over, let the mainsheet out until the boat comes level. Don't forget to pull the mainsheet in again as the gust passes, or the boat will heel over on top of you.

Don't let the gust turn the boat round into the wind. Be firm with the tiller and keep the boat going in the direction *you* want.

Sail controls

The sail should be set so there is a good curve or belly in the sail.

The kicking strap (vang) should be 'normal' (see page 15).

The cunningham should be loose. Let the rope off until creases appear along the front edge of the sail. Then pull in the rope until the creases just disappear.

The sail outhaul should be loose. You should be able to get your fist between the foot of the sail and the middle of the boom.

In stronger winds, all three sail controls should be tighter. In light winds, the sail controls should be looser.

Going faster

If you want to win races, it's esential to be able to reach fast. Here are some points to watch and some ideas to try.

- Keep the boat absolutely upright.

- Adjust the mainsheet all the time.

- Use your body weight. Hike out as far as you can. Move back in gusts, forward in lulls. If the boat heels, try to bring it upright with your weight before letting out the mainsheet.

- Steer a straight course. Don't weave about – the rudder acts as a brake each time you use it.

- In a strong gust, alter course away from the wind, easing the mainsheet. Get back on course when the gust has passed.

- Turn away from the wind each time a wave picks up the boat. Try to surf on each wave.

- Try pushing a length of wool through your sail about 30 cm back from the mast. When the sail is properly adjusted, the wool should stream back on both sides of the sail. If the sail is too far in, the leeward 'woolly' will collapse; too far out, and the windward one will collapse.

The photograph above shows good reaching technique. The helmsman is using his weight to keep the boat absolutely level. His attention is on the front part of the sail (as well as where he's going!) and he continually adjusts the mainsheet. Because the boat is level, he can steer gently and easily. The kicking strap (vang) is tight, but the other controls are loose. The sail has a good curve in it for maximum power.

As you become more experienced you will find it helpful to take the mainsheet straight from the boom to your hand (cutting out the mainsheet block). This gives a more positive response.

Reaching in light winds

Reaching in light winds needs patience. Try to keep still – if the boat rocks about the wind is 'shaken' out of the sail.

Above: In light winds, sit well forward and heel the boat to windward to cut down the wetted area of the hull (left). If the sail falls out of shape you may need to heel the boat to leeward so that gravity keeps the sail full (right).

Trim
Sit right forward to lift the stern of the boat clear of the water. This cuts down the wetted area of the hull and hence the friction between the hull and the water.

Heel the boat to windward or leeward. This cuts down the wetted area of the hull even further. In really light winds, you may need to hold the boom out to keep the sail full and the air flowing over it.

Sail controls
The cunningham and outhaul should be loose. The kicking strap (vang) should be slightly looser than 'normal'. Aim for a lot of curve in the sail.

Steering
Hold the tiller extension gently and try to alter course as little as possible. If the boat is stopped, you can turn it by 'pumping' – pull on the tiller hard then push it back gently. Repeat several times (but not when you are racing!).

Gusts
Change course away from the wind and try to stay with the gust as long as possible. Then get back on or above your course and wait for the next gust.

Burgee
In light winds, it's important to keep an eye on your burgee and the ripples on the water to spot changes in wind direction.

Reaching in strong winds

Reaching in a good breeze is the ultimate in Laser sailing. It's amazing how fast the boat can go, particularly down waves. At these high speeds the helmsman must act fast and firmly.

Adjusting the sail
Hike out hard, then pull the sail in as far as you can while keeping the boat level. Keep steering in a straight line, 'playing' the mainsheet to keep the boat upright. In a gust, let out the mainsheet.

Steering
Don't let the boat turn through too big an angle, or 'centrifugal' force will capsize it.

Remember that each time you push the tiller the boat will turn into the wind and heel away from you. When you pull the tiller the boat will turn away from the wind and heel over on top of you. By adjusting both mainsheet and tiller every couple of seconds you can keep the boat upright and go really fast.

Try to steer down waves as much as possible. As a wave picks up the boat, turn away from the wind and surf down the wave.

Trim
Hike at the back of the cockpit (if your toe straps are adjustable, tighten them). This lets the bow of the boat come up and skim over the water – this is *planing*.

Gusts
Don't let a gust slew the boat round into the wind. If you do, the quick turn will send you swimming. As a gust hits, let the sail out slightly and turn 10° to 20° away from the wind. This lets the boat 'ride with the punch'. Try to keep breathing, despite the spray!

If the boat rolls, pull the sail in and use your weight to 'dampen' the roll. Check that the centreboard is half down. In a real squall, keep on a reach with most of the sail flapping.

Sail controls
To cut down on adjustments, keep the outhaul and cunningham very tight all round the course. But if you have been super-vanging on the beat you must release the kicking strap on the reach or the boom may break.

Below: A loose kicking strap (vang) lets the sail twist too much. Tighten the kicking strap until the top batten is parallel to the boom (right).

Below: On a reach tighten the toe straps to keep your bottom out of the water.

Above: Common mistakes – the sail controls have been pulled too tight and there is no power in the sail. Note the creases at mast and boom.

Above: Common mistakes – this boat was allowed to slew round into the wind as a gust hit. The speed of the turn has caused a capsize.

Below: Common mistakes – the burgee indicates that this boat is reaching, but the mainsheet has been pulled in too far.

Below: Common mistakes – the mainsheet is too far out. The helmsman should hike, and pull the mainsheet in until the sail stops flapping.

9 Beating

Beating in a Laser, particularly in a blow, is one of the most satisfying parts of sailing. You are, literally, beating the wind which is trying to push you back.

What is beating?
A boat cannot sail straight into the wind (from A to B in the diagram). The sail will flap, and the boat will be blown backwards. The only way is to beat – to sail a zigzag course at an angle of about 45° to the wind.

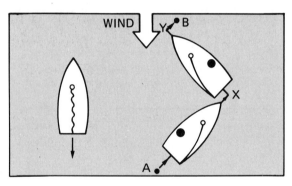

Steering
To beat, pull in the mainsheet until the mainsheet block and boom end block are touching; hike out, and steer as close to the wind as you can. The course is a compromise: if you steer too close to the wind you slow down, even though you are pointing closer to B. If you steer too far from the wind, you go faster, but are pointing well away from B.

The simplest check on your course is to watch the front of the sail. Turn towards the wind until the sail begins to flap, then turn back until it just stops flapping. You are now on course. Repeat this every few seconds – both to check your course, and because the wind constantly changes its direction.

At points X and Y the boat tacks through about 90°. Tacking is discussed on page 35.

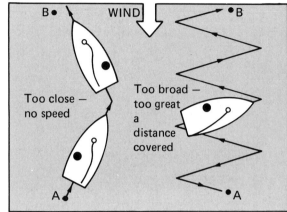

Adjusting the traveller
In medium and strong winds, pull the traveller in tight. In light winds, let it off a few centimetres to bring the boom nearer the centre of the boat.

Adjusting the sail
When beating in medium or light winds there is no need to adjust the mainsheet. Keep it pulled in, and concentrate on using the tiller to keep the boat at the proper angle to the wind. Ideally you won't cleat the sheet, but if you must, keep the loose part in your hand so you can release it in a gust.

The tension on the mainsheet is important. In medium winds, pull it in until the mainsheet and boom end blocks are touching. In light and in very strong winds, you will need to let the mainsheet out a little.

Trim
Sit at the front end of the cockpit. Hike to keep the boat absolutely upright.

Centreboard
The centreboard should be pushed right down when beating to prevent the boat slipping sideways through the water.

If the kicking strap (vang) is loose the boom will rise when you let out the mainsheet.

With a tight kicking strap the boom moves out horizontally: just what you want.

Gusts

The water looks dark as a gust travels over it. As the gust hits you, hike out hard and turn into the wind a few degrees. If the boat still heels, let the sail out a little. When the boat has picked up speed, pull the sail in again. When the gust has passed, move your weight inboard and adjust your course as necessary.

Sail controls

The sail should be set flatter than when reaching or running.

The kicking strap (vang) should be 'normal' or, in strong winds, tighter than normal.

The cunningham should be completely slack in light winds. Begin to pull it on when you are fully hiked. In strong winds, pull it very tight.

The sail outhaul should be adjusted according to your weight, to the wind strength and to the wave conditions. If you are overpowered, pull the outhaul tighter. If not, loosen it to put a bit of curve in the bottom of the sail. Too much curve stops the boat pointing close to the wind (because the 'bag' in the sail flaps). Too little curve means the sail has no power, and the boat loses speed. Try to get a 'compromise' setting. In waves, you need a slacker outhaul to give the boat power to get over the crests.

Going faster

Most races start with a beat and it's essential to get to the first mark well up in the fleet. Here are some points to watch and some ideas to try:

- Keep the boat absolutely upright.

- Keep the mainsheet pulled in 'block to block' except in light and very strong winds.

- Hike as hard as you can. Only let the sail out as a last resort.

- Watch the front of the sail like a hawk. Keep altering course so the sail just doesn't flap.

- Don't slam the bow into waves.

- Watch out for windshifts.

- Keep a good lookout for other boats (particularly by watching underneath the sail).

Beating in light winds

Aim for speed rather than steering very close to the wind. Keep an eye on the water and on your burgee to spot windshifts.

Adjusting the traveller
Ease the traveller slightly so the traveller block can run over the tiller. Let out the mainsheet slightly so that the blocks are 20 to 30 cm apart.

Adjusting the sail
Keep the mainsheet in your hand. There is no need to cleat it in light winds. When a gust comes, let the mainsheet out a little. As the boat gathers speed, pull the mainsheet back in. Don't pull the mainsheet too tight – you are aiming for speed through the water, not to sail a course very close to the wind.

Steering
Hold the tiller extension gently. Watch the front of the sail and steer as close to the wind as you can without the sail flapping. You will find you

Below: In light winds, get right forward to lift the stern. Heel to leeward to fill the sail.

need to alter course every few seconds to keep 'on the wind'.

Trim
Sit on the foredeck and heel the boat to leeward. Both actions cut down the wetted area of the hull. (The Laser racing rules prevent your having any part of your body in front of the mast.) You may find you need a longer tiller extension to let you get right forward.

Sail controls
Set the kicking strap (vang) at least as tight as normal. This bends the mast and gives a better shape to the sail.

The cunningham should be loose; don't worry about creases in the front of the sail.

The sail outhaul should be loose (about 20 cm between the foot of the sail and the middle of the boom).

Beating in strong winds

In these conditions both the wind and the waves tend to stop the boat. You must not let this happen because you can only steer when the boat is moving – so speed through the waves is your main aim.

Adjusting the traveller
Pull the traveller as tight as possible. This lets the traveller block slide out further.

Adjusting the sail
Try to beat with the mainsheet pulled in as tight as possible. This bends the mast, reducing the curve in the sail. To keep the boat level, you will have to point close to the wind – the front part of the sail will flap all the time.

In very strong winds the boat may stop if you use this technique. In this case make sure the kicking strap (vang) is very tight, then let out the mainsheet as much as is needed to keep the boat moving fast enough for you to steer properly. The front of the sail will be flapping a little as you 'reach' to windward.

Centreboard
In very strong winds, pull the centreboard up 10 to 20 cm. This lets the boat slide sideways and 'ride with the punch'.

Hiking
Your body weight provides the power to drive to windward. The more you hike, the faster you go. Adjust the toe strap so you're comfortable. If you trail in the water, or if your shins hurt, tighten the toe strap; otherwise, loosen it so you can get further outboard.

Trim
In large waves, move about halfway back in the cockpit. This lets the bow ride over the waves. Try leaning towards the stern as the boat goes up a wave, and forwards as it goes down.

Steering over waves
Try to steer so the boat has an easy passage over the waves. As the bow goes up a wave, push the tiller away a little. Pull the tiller as the bow reaches the crest, and turn away down the back of the wave. Repeat this for each wave – you will find you're moving the tiller all the time. Keep hiking as hard as you can.

Gusts
Let the mainsheet out as much as is necessary to keep the boat moving.

Sail controls
The kicking strap (vang), cunningham and outhaul should all be bar tight.

Below: In strong winds, sit halfway down the cockpit and hike out hard.

Above: Common mistakes – the sail controls are too loose. Note the curve in the kicking strap (vang) and the creases halfway up the sail.

Above: Common mistakes – this boat is steering too far from the wind. That is why it is heeling so much.

Below: Common mistakes – this boat is heeling too much because of the helmsman's reluctance to hike. Keep the boat level!

Below: Common mistakes – the mainsheet is too loose. This prevents the boat sailing close to the wind and does not bend the mast enough.

What is tacking?

The boat in the diagram is beating with the wind on the starboard side (a). The boat turns into the wind (b), and keeps turning until it is beating with the wind on the port side (c). The turn is called a tack.

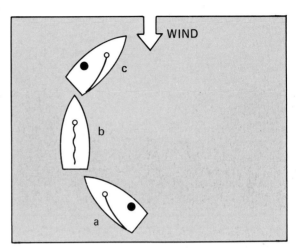

Six steps to a good tack

1 *Get some speed*. Hike extra hard to get the boat moving as fast as possible. You will need this speed to turn 'through' the wind and waves. Uncleat the mainsheet. Let the boat heel a little to leeward.

2 *Turn*. Still hiking, and with the mainsheet still pulled in, push the tiller away from you. Push gently at first, then a little harder. Keep the tiller pushed over until step 5.

3 *Cross the boat*. As the boat begins to roll on top of you, dive across it facing forwards. You will land on the new side with the tiller behind your back and the mainsheet across your body. (Moving across the boat automatically lets the mainsheet out a little – this allows the traveller block to move across to the other side of the traveller).

4 *Straighten up*. As you land on the new side put your front foot under the toestrap and begin to straighten up. Don't let the boat spin round too far (on to a reach) – you are trying to get to windward.

5 *Change hands*. Sail with the tiller behind your back until the boat has settled down. Then bring your mainsheet hand across the front of your body and grab the tiller with it. Lastly, transfer your 'old' tiller hand to the mainsheet, and swivel the tiller extension forward across your body.

6 *Hike*. Pull in the mainsheet, put your back foot under the toestrap, hike out and go.

Get some speed . . .   *Turn . . .*

Land on the other side . . .   *Straighten up and change hands . . .*

Duck down . . .   *Dive across the boat facing forwards . . .*

Gather up the mainsheet . . .   *Swivel the extension forward, and go!*

Above: Common mistakes – this helmsman has straightened up too early: the boat has turned halfway and stopped.

Below: Common mistakes – don't let out too much mainsheet as you turn.

Above: Common mistakes – don't change sides too early. Wait until the boat is pointing into the wind. Swivel the tiller extension forwards.

Below: Common mistakes – remember to tack facing forwards!

What is running?
Both boats in the diagram are running – they are sailing with the wind directly behind them.

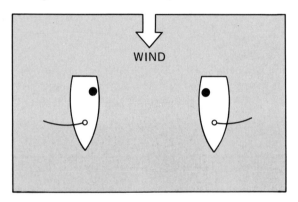

WIND

Adjusting the sail
In medium and light winds, the mainsheet should be as far out as possible. In strong winds, when the boat tends to roll, pull the mainsheet in a little – but remember that the boat goes faster with the sail right out. Don't forget to tie a knot in the end of the mainsheet, or it may slip out through the block.

Centreboard
Pull the centreboard three-quarters of the way up. In very strong winds, push the centreboard further down to dampen rolling. Never have the centreboard right down when running, and never take the centreboard out – this creates too much turbulence in the centreboard box.

Trim
Except in light winds, sit towards the back of the cockpit. The wind tends to push the bow down on a run, and your weight near the stern helps counteract this.

There is no need to hike on a run. Sit near the centreline, with one foot braced against each side of the cockpit, and be ready to move your weight either way. Watch out that the tiller doesn't catch on your thigh; think ahead so you don't have to make violent tiller movements.

Heeling the boat to windward helps you steer without using too much rudder.

Steering
Avoid violent turns – the boat is travelling fast and 'centrifugal' force will capsize you. Aim to

turn smoothly and slowly.

It is vital to avoid an unexpected gybe (gybing is discussed on page 45). Watch the burgee carefully and avoid turning so that the wind is blowing from the same side as the boom. This is

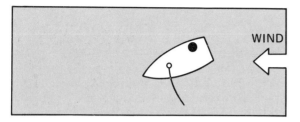

'running by the lee'·– the wind is able to get behind the boom and flip it across. If you find yourself in this position, push the tiller away from you for a moment. Then straighten up.

Gusts

Keep going, even in strong gusts. Don't let the gust turn the boat round into the wind – keep a straight course. If the boat rolls, pull in the mainsheet. If the boat heels away from you, let the mainsheet out. If it heels towards you, pull the mainsheet in.

Sail controls

The kicking strap (vang) should be 'normal' except in light winds, when it should be slacker than normal.

The cunningham and sail outhaul should be loose. Aim for a lot of curve in the sail.

Going faster

You can often gain a good number of places on a run, particularly if you are towards the back of the fleet and the wind comes up. Those in front

are at your mercy because you can blanket them from the wind. Here are some points to watch:

- Let the mainsheet out as far as possible.
- Make sure you have the centreboard well up.
- When a gust comes, run straight down wind with it. Try to stay with the gust as long as possible. If you see a gust to one side of the course, sail over to it and then ride it.
- Try to surf on waves as much as you can. Pull the mainsheet in a little as the boat accelerates down each wave.

Right: Heel the boat to windward until you can steer easily. If the boat rolls further towards you push on the tiller and haul in the mainsheet (below right); if it heels away from you pull on the tiller and let out the mainsheet (below).

Running in light winds

Trim
Sit as far forward as you can, holding the boom out. You may like to push the centreboard down to make this position more comfortable – though this will lose you some speed.

In very light winds, heel the boat to leeward to help keep the boom out and to put some shape in the sail. Otherwise, heel the boat to windward.

Steering
Use the tiller as little as possible.

Sail controls
The kicking strap (vang) should be slacker than 'normal' – this allows the mast to straighten and puts more curve in the sail. The cunningham and sail outhaul should be loose.

Mainsheet
Try to encourage the wind to flow over the sail by letting out the boom more than 90°. You can then heel the boat to windward which keeps the boom out and the mainsheet tight.

Running in strong winds

Steering
Don't be in a hurry to get on a run when the wind is really blowing. Pull the centreboard half

Below: In light airs let the sail out more than 90°: you can then heel the boat to windward which improves steering. If the mainsheet is too short for this, heel the boat to leeward (left).

up before you begin. Then steer round gradually from a reach; hike out and let out the sail slowly as you turn. Move back to lift the bow.

As you come on to the run the boat will move really fast. If it starts to roll, immediately pull in a little mainsheet. Keep a firm hand on the tiller, and don't let the boat slew round onto a reach. On the other hand, don't turn so far that you run by the lee.

The tiller is the main means of keeping the boat upright. If the boat heels towards you, push the tiller away a little (and pull in the mainsheet). Then straighten up. If the boat heels away from you pull the tiller towards you (and let out the mainsheet). You will find you need to keep the sheet and tiller in constant motion down a hairy run.

Try to sail down the waves. As a wave comes up behind, turn away from the wind and surf on the wave. If you shoot down it and the bow

Below: Former world champion Lawrence Crispin powers down the run.

looks as though it's going to hit the wave in front, turn into the wind a little and try to climb the new wave. If you're overtaking the waves, you're really going fast!

Adjusting the sail
Keep the mainsheet as far out as possible without the boat rolling. It may help to move the knot in the mainsheet to keep it in this position. Then, if you accidentally let go of the mainsheet all may not be lost. If the worst happens keep hold of the mainsheet as you go over the side. Then use it to pull yourself back to the capsized boat.

Centreboard
Keep the centreboard half down. But if you start rolling horribly, try pushing the board right down until you are stable again.

Sail controls
In strong winds it's best to leave everything tight, although experts let off the cunningham and the kicking strap (vang).

Above: Common mistakes – don't let the boat heel to leeward: let out the mainsheet.

Below: Common mistakes – if the boat rolls, pull in the mainsheet!

Above: Common mistakes – the centreboard is too far down for efficiency.

Below: Common mistakes – the kicking strap (vang) is loose, so there is too much sail twist.

What is gybing?
In the diagram below, boat (a) is running with the sail on the starboard side. The helmsman turns through a small angle (b). The wind forces the sail out to the port side of the boat (c). The turn is called a *gybe*.

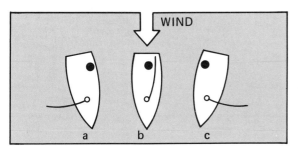

Why is gybing difficult?
Gybing is the hardest sailing manoeuvre. Unlike tacking, the wind pushes on the sail throughout the turn. The boat is moving at high speed, so it is very sensitive to tiller movements. A miscalculation results in the boat rolling – with the sail 'edge on' there's not much to dampen the roll and the helmsman tends to take an involuntary dip.

Decide when you want to gybe, and then do it! The best moment is when the boat is moving fast down a wave – since you're travelling away from the wind, the 'push' on the sail is lessened.

Six steps to a good gybe

1 *Get ready*. Push the centreboard half down (this is vital). Take the mainsheet (in your front hand) straight from the boom. Turn the boat until the wind is almost directly behind, and make sure the boat is flat. (It is impossible to gybe if the boat is heeling away from you.)

2 *Pull in the mainsheet*. Pull in an arm's length of mainsheet, and move your hand so the rope is tight (later you will want to jerk the sheet).

3 *Turn*. Heel the boat towards you (which helps the boat turn). Firmly but slowly, pull the tiller extension towards you.

4 *Cross the boat*. Look at the burgee to see when you are dead downwind. At this point the boat slows; jerk the mainsheet to start the boom moving and cross the boat facing forwards. Don't forget to duck!

5 *Steer*. As you land on the new side, pull the tiller towards you. This stops the boat turning through too large an angle. You should find yourself sitting with the tiller behind your back and the mainsheet held across your body.

6 *Smile*. You made it! If the boat rolls, pull in the mainsheet; otherwise let it out to the normal racing position. Finally, when the boat is under control, change hands on the tiller and the mainsheet and bring the tiller extension across your body.

Gybing in very strong winds
In very strong winds a capsize may be inevitable. If you *know* you are going to capsize, it's better to wear round. This involves turning the boat through 360°. Do this with the centreboard half up. Pull in the mainsheet and spin the boat around fast.

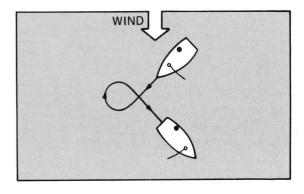

Haul in the mainsheet . . .   *Pull the tiller towards you . . .*   *Turn . . .*

Land on the other side . . .   *Adjust the mainsheet . . .*

Jerk the mainsheet . . .   *Duck!*   *Cross the boat . . .*

Change hands . . .   *Sort out the tiller and go!*

Above: Common mistakes – pull the tiller towards you at the end of the gybe, or you will go on turning and may capsize.

Below: Common mistakes – pull in some mainsheet before you gybe – this helmsman will have to turn a long way before the sail flips over.

Above: Common mistakes – remember to tweak the mainsheet as the boom slams across, or the slack will catch round the back of the boat.

Below: Common mistakes – if the centreboard is too far down it 'locks' the hull in the water and gives the sail a pivot to act on.

Everyone capsizes. Indeed if you don't capsize sometimes, you're not really trying.

When the inevitable happens, try to stay on top of the boat. In most other classes, the crew needs to swim to right the boat. In the Laser this is unnecessary.

Never leave the boat (to swim for the shore, for example). The hull will support you almost indefinitely and it is more easily spotted than a swimmer.

Capsizing to leeward

Try to turn round as the boat capsizes so you are facing 'uphill'. Climb over the side and on to the centreboard. Lean in and make sure the centreboard is fully down and the mainsheet is uncleated. Then lean back and slowly pull the boat upright. If you do this slowly, the boat automatically turns into the wind. At the last moment, straddle the deck and scramble into the cockpit.

1 *The boat capsizes to windward . . .*

2 *Pull yourself back along the mainsheet . . .*

3 *Stand on the lip of the hull . . .*

4 *Climb onto the centreboard . . .*

5 *Clamber over the side . . .*

6 *Get in – fast!*

Above: Recovering from a capsize to leeward – without getting wet.

Even if the boat turns upside down, this is no problem in a Laser. Climb on to the hull, stand on the 'lip' at the edge of the boat *with your back to the wind* and pull the boat on to its side. Scramble on to the centreboard and right the boat as before.

Avoiding a capsize to leeward
- Watch for gusts.
- Keep the mainsheet in your hand at all times while sailing.
- Hike in strong winds.
- On a reach or run, avoid letting the boat turn fast into the wind.

Capsizing to windward
Try to stay on top of the boat. However, you may well fall out as the boat capsizes to windward. If this happens on a reach or run, hang on to the mainsheet at all costs – the boat is travelling fast and may finish up some distance away. The mainsheet is your lifeline. *Do not* hang on to the tiller extension which may snap as you go over the side.

1 Pull yourself back to the boat along the mainsheet. Make sure that it is uncleated. Climb over the side of the boat on to the centreboard.
2 Gently lever the mast out of the water. As the wind picks it up, straddle the side deck. As the boat begins to come upright, get your body into the cockpit and across to the windward side. You need to move very fast to prevent the boat capsizing again to leeward.

3 If the boat does capsize again, go over the side on to the centreboard once more, and right the boat as for a capsize to leeward.

In *shallow water*, don't let the boat turn upside down or the mast may snap.

If the mast gets stuck in mud, stand on the centreboard close to the hull and gently bounce up and down to free it.

Avoiding a capsize to windward
- Be ready to move your weight inboard in lulls.
- Pull in the mainsheet rapidly if the boat rolls to windward.
- On a reach or run, avoid turning fast away from the wind.

If at first you don't succeed . . .

You can do a good deal of damage to the boat (and even to yourself) by landing badly. The way you land will depend on the direction of the wind, but two points always apply:

- Undo the rudder downhaul and the centreboard shockcord in good time.

- Push up the self bailer.

Landing with the wind along the shore
This is the easiest wind direction for landing.

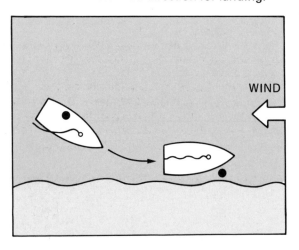

1 Sail slowly towards the shore. Control the boat's speed with the mainsheet, letting it out as you approach to slow the boat down.

2 At the last minute, take out the centreboard and turn into the wind.

3 Step into the water on the shore side of the boat, holding it as near the bow as you can.

4 Make sure the mainsheet is free. Slacken the kicking strap (vang).

5 If you are on a sandy shore, leave the boat aground while you get your trolley. If there are rocks, ask someone else to get your trolley for you while you hold the boat.

Landing with an offshore wind
Beat in towards the shore. On the approach leg (A in the diagram) control the speed with the mainsheet. At the last moment take out the

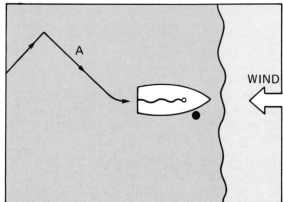

centreboard, turn the boat into the wind and step into the water as near the bow as you can. Then proceed as above.

Landing with an onshore wind.
This is the most difficult direction for landing, because the wind is pushing you onshore fast.

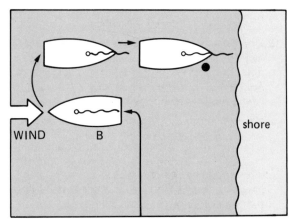

Above: Landing in an onshore wind with the knot in the mainsheet untied.

Unless the waves are very big, land as follows:

1 Sail parallel to the shore, about 30 metres out.

2 Turn into the wind (B in the diagram) and unclip the mainsheet and traveller blocks. If your blocks are taped together, undo the knot in either end of the mainsheet.

3 Point the boat towards the shore and let it drift in. The sail will blow forwards; the wind pressure on the mast is all that is pushing the boat ashore. If you are still going too fast trail a leg in the water as a brake.

4 At the last minute, take out the centreboard and step into the water.

Landing in very shallow water

Come in slowly. Lift up the rudder blade in good time and step into the water early.

Landing in big waves and an onshore wind

The method described above won't work in very large waves, because of the danger that a wave may roll the boat over. Use the following technique instead.

1 While well offshore, undo the rudder downhaul and push it into the cleat. The rudder blade will come up when it hits the beach. Don't pull up the blade – you need all the control you can get. Pull the centreboard three-quarters up.

2 As you get near the beach, choose the smallest wave you can find and surf full speed on it towards the beach. Keep the bow pointing straight at the shore. Sit well back to let the bow ride up the beach. As the boat grounds, jump out and drag the boat up the beach. Don't get to leeward of the boat or a wave may push it into you with painful results.

Landing at a jetty

Sail toward the jetty slowly, controlling your speed with the mainsheet. Turn into the wind at the last moment.

If the 'ideal' position (C in the diagram) is occupied, follow course D. As the boat turns into the wind, go forward (by heeling the boat and slipping round the mast) and grab the jetty. You can crouch on the foredeck while you tie up.

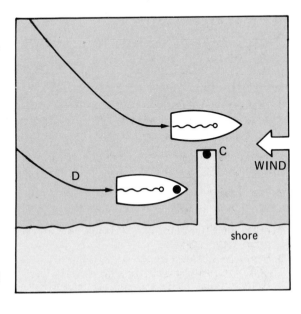

15 Other rigs

The standard Laser can be a bit of a handful for light sailors, so two alternative rigs have been developed. The clever bit is that all the normal gear is used – the only difference is the sail and the lower mast section.

The standard Laser has a 7.06 square metre sail and is recommended for helmsmen weighing more than 65 kg (140 lb). The Laser Radial has a shorter bottom mast and a 5.76 square metre sail, and is recommended for those weighing 55–65 kg (120–140 lb). The Laser 4.7 has a 4.7 square metre sail and a shorter lower mast which is permanently bent to keep the boat balanced. The rig is ideal for those weighing 35–55 kg (77–120 lb).

Races are held for each rig. They can, of course, be raced against each other informally, but not in major regattas.

The various rigs are particularly useful for families with growing children: they can start off in a 4.7, then progress to the Radial or standard Laser simply by changing the bottom mast section and sail.

Below: Lightweight performance with the Laser 4.7 (left) and the Laser Radial (right).

16   Looking after your Laser

Here are a few do's and don'ts about boat maintenance.

- DO keep your boat clean – use soap or detergent but *not* any abrasive substance. Difficult stains are removable with xylene or acetone, but the area should be drenched with fresh water immediately afterwards.
- DO support the hull at the strongest points – the mast position and just inside the rear end of the cockpit. Use these points whichever way up the boat is.

  The Laser is best stored deck up, although it is more stable on the car roof-rack deck down.

  The best anchorage points for tying down are the bow eye and the traveller fairleads – not the gudgeons!
- DO empty water from the hull after use. An inspection hatch is useful both for airing the hull and for access. Leave the hatch and the transom drain bung open when the boat is not is use.
- DO store your boat away from direct sunlight and use a cover. A few coats of wax will inhibit sun fade and make cleaning easier.
- DO check the tightness of all your fittings regularly. The gooseneck, rudder head bolt and the screws holding deck fittings need constant attention. Check the rivets holding the mainsheet blocks to the boom, and replace if loose.
- DO keep your spars free from abrasion. A good coat of wax will allow the sail to slide up and down easily in response to your cunningham adjustments.
- DO remember that a fibreglass hull can take on weight with age or neglect at nearly the same rate as a wooden one. Look after it by keeping it dry, aired and sheltered from the weather when not in use.
- After sailing in salt water, DO hose down the entire boat and sail in fresh water. Corrosion attacks metal quickly, so pay special attention to metal fittings and the insides of your boom and lower mast.
- DO fold your sail. The folds should be parallel to the boom. Make the folds in different places each time and avoid folds across the window.
- DO replace the plug at the bottom of the mast if the grooves have disappeared with wear. (Grit can sit in these grooves – in their absence the mast and grit act like a drill head and drill through the hull.)
- DON'T subject your hull to abnormal point loadings, whether in storage or on an unsuitable trolley or trailer.
- DON'T leave your hull on any water-susceptible surface such as sand, grass or carpet.
- DON'T leave your boat unattended when rigged – it may capsize and suffer damage.
- DON'T forget to tie down your hull – it is very light and may blow away.
- DON'T leave your centreboard in excessively hot conditions, such as in a car, especially if it's not supported evenly along its entire length.

  Chips on the centreboard and rudder can be repaired with wood and an epoxy glue. Dents and scratches can be rubbed down and filled but if the high-tensile wire reinforcement is exposed any rust must be removed before filling. Finally, repaint using two-part polyurethane.
- DON'T wash your sail in hot water or a washing machine, or try to iron it. Above all, don't leave it to flog or even flutter for any longer than you can help.
- DON'T seal the breathing hole under the forward end of the toe strap (hiking strap).
- DON'T paint your hull. You will add at least 2kg of unnecessary weight and will compromise the resale value. Scratches on fibreglass always look worse than they are: most scratches can be filled or simply polished out.

17 Racing

The rules

A full discussion of the rules is outside the scope of this book. For the cautious beginner, a few key rules will keep him out of trouble.

Boats meeting on opposite tacks

A boat is either on a port tack or a starboard tack. It is on a port tack when its sail is on the starboard side. In Fig. 1, boats A, B and C are on port tack; boats D, E and F are on starboard tack.

A port tack boat must keep clear of a starboard tack boat.

D, E and F have right of way over A, B and C, who must keep clear.

Boats meeting on the same tack

If the boats are overlapped (if the bow of the following boat is ahead of a line at right angles to the stern of the leading boat) the following rule applies:

A windward boat shall keep clear of a leeward boat.

In Fig. 2, G must keep clear of H, I must keep clear of J and L must keep clear of K.

If the boats are not overlapped (Fig. 3):

A boat clear astern shall keep clear of a boat clear ahead.

If M is sailing faster he is not allowed to sail into the back of N.

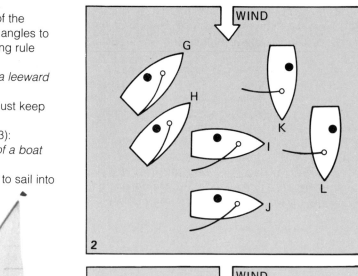

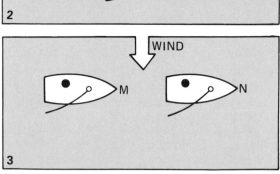

Boats meeting at marks

An outside boat shall give each boat overlapping it on the inside room to round or pass the mark.

P must give O room to round the mark on the inside. O must get his overlap on P before P's bow reaches an imaginary circle of radius two boat's lengths from the mark (Fig. 4). In

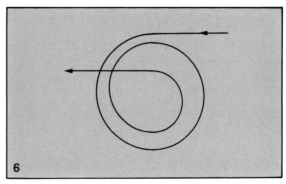

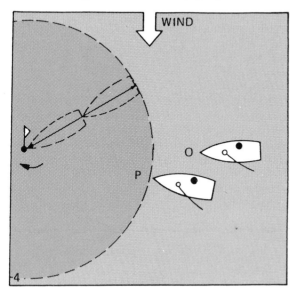

simplest method). Argue your case in the protest room afterwards.

If you hit another boat and are in the wrong you may exonerate yourself by sailing clear and doing a 720 degree turn. You have to include two tacks and two gybes (Fig. 6).

If you hit a mark sail well clear of the other boats, do a 360 degree turn then sail on (see Fig. 7).

Fig. 5, the boats are rounding the buoy to port (anticlockwise). The boat nearest the camera has the right to turn inside the other boat.

Note that this rule does not apply at starts (see page 58).

Penalties

If you hit another boat and reckon you're in the right, protest by flying a red flag (a small piece of cloth clothespegged to your kicking strap is the

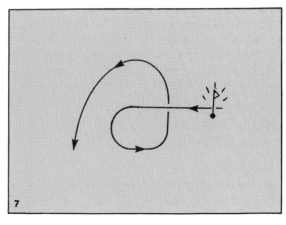

The start

The start is the most important part of the race. If you get a bad start, you have to overtake everyone to win; while you're battling past the opposition, the leaders are sailing further ahead. If you get a good start, you're sailing in clear air.

How is a race started?

Most races are started on a beat. The race committee sets a start line (Fig. 8), usually between the mast of the committee boat (A) and a buoy (B). They often lay another buoy (C), which does not have to be on the line. Boats are not allowed to sail between C and A.

Ten minutes before the start the class flag (or a white shape) is raised on the committee boat and a gun is fired.

Five minutes before the start the Blue Peter (or a blue shape) is raised and gun is fired.

At the start, both flags are lowered (or a red shape is raised) and a gun is fired.

Boats must be behind the start line when the starting gun is fired. Your aim is to be just behind the line, sailing at full speed, when the gun fires.

How can I get a good start?

Set your watch at the ten-minute gun, and check it at the five-minute gun.

During the last few minutes, avoid the 'danger' areas X and Y. From X you cannot get on to the start line because the boats to leeward have right of way. Boat D, for example, will be forced the wrong side of buoy C. In Y you are bound to pass the wrong side of buoy B. Boat F has this problem.

Don't go too far from the line – 30 metres is plenty. A wall of boats builds up on the line in the last two minutes, and you must be in that wall. If you're behind it, not only can you not get in, but your wind is cut off by the wall.

Aim to be three or four boat lengths behind the line with 45 seconds to go. Control your speed very carefully using the mainsheet. Keep

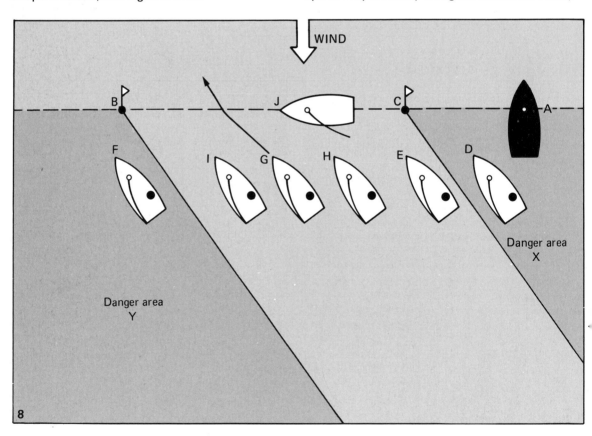

the boat creeping forward as slowly as you can –
most of the sail will be flapping. With five seconds
to go, you should be one length behind the line.
Pull in the mainsheet, hike out and start beating.
You should cross the line just after the gun with
full speed. Boat G has followed this advice.

What about the other boats?
It's important to watch out for other boats as
you line up to start. G has right of way over H,
but must keep clear of I. As you line up, keep
turning into the wind a little. This keeps you
away from the boat to leeward – it also open up
a nice 'hole' to leeward that you can sail down
into at the start (for extra speed).

Don't reach down the line with 15 seconds to
go like boat J. You will have no rights over G, H
and I who will sail into you. If you're too early,
let the sail out in good time and slow down.

Which end of the line should I start?
In Fig. 8 the wind is at right angles to the start
line. In this case it doesn't matter where you
start – the middle of the line is as good as
anywhere.

Usually, however, the wind is not at right
angles to the line. You can find out what it's
doing by sailing down the line on a reach. Adjust
the sail so the front just flaps (Fig. 9).

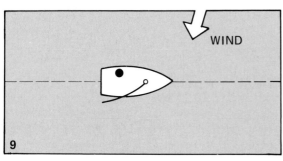

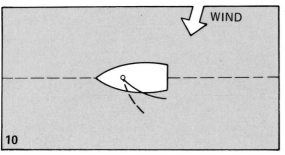

Keeping the mainsheet in the same position,
tack and reach down the line. In Fig. 10, the sail
will now be too far in – you will have to let the
mainsheet out to make it flap. This indicates the
wind is blowing from the starboard end of the
line – and you should start at this end.

How do I make a starboard end start?
Sail slowly, and as close to the wind as possible,
so you will reach the windward end of the line
with the gun (Fig. 11). Boats to windward have
no rights and are forced out. Boats to leeward
can't touch you – you are already sailing as
close to the wind as possible.

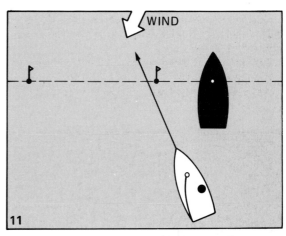

How do I make a port end start?
Keep near the port end of the line (Fig. 12). Aim
to cross as near the buoy as possible. Tack on to
port tack as soon as you can clear the fleet.

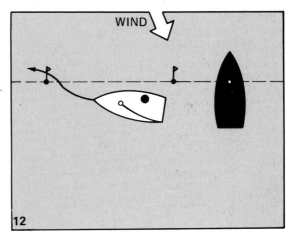

The beat

After the tension of the start, it's important to settle down and concentrate on sailing hard and fast.

What about other boats?

A boat when beating casts a 'wind shadow' – shown in Fig. 13. It also creates an area of disturbed air to windward due to the wind being deflected by the sail: the air behind the boat is also disturbed.

You should therefore avoid sailing just to windward of another boat, behind it or in its wind shadow. In the diagram, boat B should either tack or bear away to clear its wind. Boats D and F should both tack.

Which way should I go?

You may have to modify your course to take account of tides and windshifts, but your first aim should be to make reasonably long tacks to start with, shortening them as you approach the windward mark.

Don't sail into the area indicated by the shaded part of Fig. 14 – if you do, you will have to reach in to the buoy and will lose valuable time and distance. Stay inside the lay lines – these are the paths you would sail when beating to hit the windward mark.

For safety's sake, arrange your tacks so that you come into the mark on starboard tack. This gives you right of way over boats approaching on port tack, and this could be very useful when you meet at the mark.

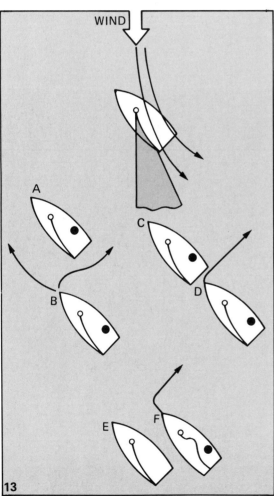

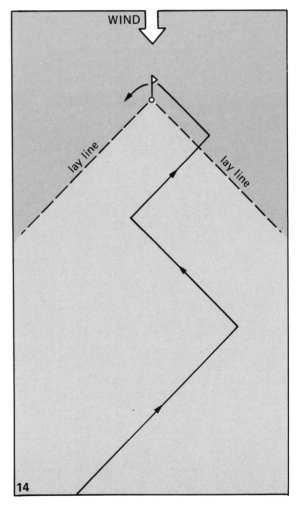

Windshifts

Once you are confident at beating and can tack efficiently, you are ready to start using windshifts.

The wind constantly alters in direction about its mean. Some of the shifts are more pronounced and last longer than others – it is these that you have to spot and use.

In shifty winds, stay close to the middle of the beat. Tack each time the wind heads you (forces you to alter course *away* from the mark). In Fig. 15, the boat takes no account of windshifts. Note how little progess it makes compared with the boat in Fig. 16, which tacks each time the wind heads it.

The main problem is to differentiate between a real shift and a short-lived change in the wind.

For that reason, sail on into each shift for five or ten seconds to make sure it's going to last. If a header lasts that long, tack.

If you find yourself tacking too often, or are confused, sail on one tack for a while until you're sure what the wind is doing. Remember that you lose at least a boat's length each time you tack, so there has to be a good reason to do so.

How can I get up the beat faster?

● Keep your wind clear.

● Watch for windshifts.

● Keep near the middle of the course.

● Practise tacking.

● Get fit – you can hike harder.

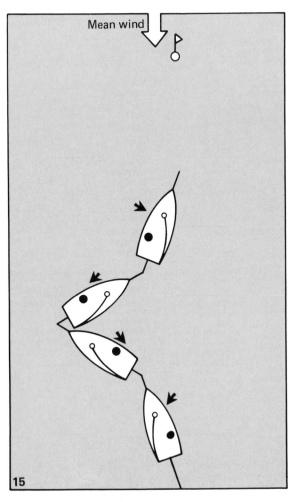

15

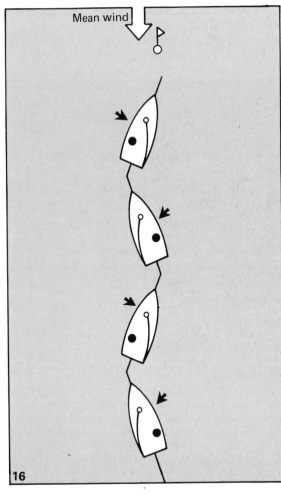

16

The reach

If it's blowing hard, pull the centreboard half up before you bear away round the windward mark. Turn slowly, moving your weight back and letting out the mainsheet.

What course should I steer?

The quickest way down the reach is a straight line from one mark to the next. However, if your rivals let you sail this course, you're lucky! The problem is that overtaking boats (A in Fig. 17) push up to windward. The boats to leeward (B) get nervous about their wind being stolen and steer high also. The result is that everyone sails an enormous arc (X) and arrives at the mark on the run, both of which cause them to lose ground on the leaders.

You have to decide whether or not to go on the 'great circle'; the alternative is to sail a leeward path (Y). You have to go down far enough to avoid the blanketing effect of the boats to windward – but usually you will sail a shorter distance than they do. You will also get the inside turn at the gybe mark. You can go for the leeward route on the second reach too, but this time you will be on the outside at the turn.

How can I get down the reach faster?

- Follow the tips for fast reaching on page 26, 'Going faster'. In particular, try to use the rudder as little as possible. Keep the boat on her feet by playing the mainsheet in and out all the time. If the boat heels or you want her to bear away, let out the mainsheet. If she comes over on top of you or you want to luff, pull in the mainsheet.

- Keep your wind clear.

- Sail the shortest route.

- Go for the inside turn at marks.

Starting the next beat

As you approach the leeward mark, tighten the cunningham and push down the centreboard. Steer round the mark so that you leave it very close (like boat C). Don't come in to the mark close (like boat D) or you'll start the beat well to leeward of your rivals.

Hike, and go!

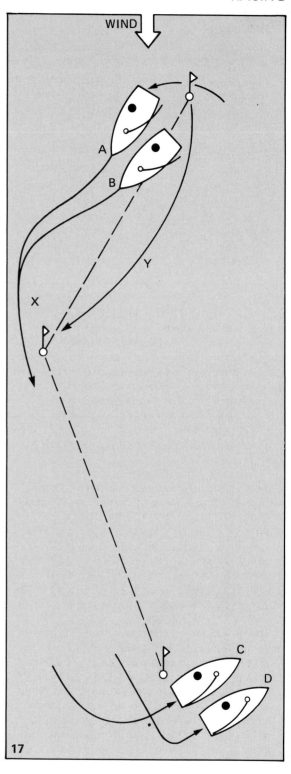

17

The run

In strong winds, take your time as you bear away on to a run. Pull the centreboard half up, sit back and adjust the mainsheet as you turn. If the boat starts to roll, steer a straight course and pull in the mainsheet a little. Continue to bear away when the boat is under control.

What course should I steer?
The quickest route is a straight line to the leeward mark (Fig. 18).

In very strong winds, you may not be able to control the boat on a straight downwind run. An alternative is to follow course Z, wearing round rather than gybing at the midpoint.

The presence of other boats may also prevent your steering a straight course. Boat F is blanketed by boat E – it can escape by steering to one side (course M or N). Other things being equal, N would be better since it gives the inside turn at the next mark.

Boat E is correct to blanket F in this way. E can attack from a range of up to four boat's lengths; it can sail right up behind F, turning to one side at the last moment to overtake. E must, of course, keep clear of F during this manoeuvre.

Watch out for boats still beating, especially when running on port tack. Alter course in good time to avoid them – a last-minute turn could capsize you.

What about crowding at the leeward mark?
It often happens that several boats arrive at the leeward mark together. The inside berth is the place to aim for – H, I and J have to give G room to turn inside them. If you're in J's position, it's better to slow down and wait to turn close to the buoy rather than sail round the outside of the pack. Try to anticipate this situation, and slow down and move across to the inside in good time. Try to get G's position.

As you get near the leeward mark, tighten the cunningham and push the centreboard down. Turn slowly and aim to leave the mark close (course O). You will need to pull in a good length of mainsheet as you round this mark – pull it in with your front hand and pass it to your tiller hand while you grab the mainsheet near the block in your front hand to pull in the next length.

How can I get down the run faster?
- Follow the 'Going faster' tips on page 40.
- Keep your wind clear.
- Sail the shortest route.
- Go for the inside turn at the leeward mark.

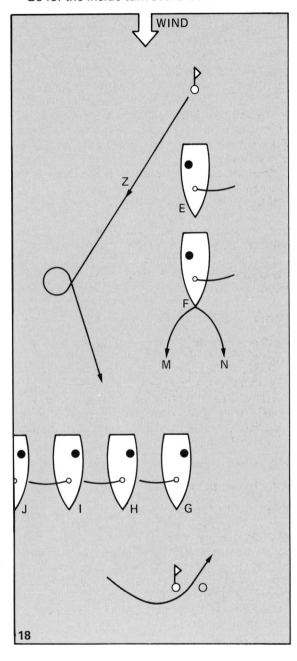

Two things will help you to enjoy your Laser more: joining a club where Lasers are raced, and joining the Laser class association. The International Laser Class Association is world wide. Its headquarters are:

> International Laser Class Association
> PO Box 26
> Falmouth
> Cornwall
> England

The ILCA is split into districts, each with its own association. By joining your local association, you automatically become a member of ILCA. If you don't know the address of your local association, write to the address above.

   The Laser association is just like a big sailing club for Laser owners. Its aims are to increase the enjoyment of Laser sailing, exchange ideas and protect the one-design principles which have made the class so popular.

- The many activities organised by the association keep the class at the front of the sailing world, which makes sure your boat will not become outdated. So there is a strong demand for second-hand Lasers and your investment is protected.

- The association produces special Laser magazines to help you understand your boat better and make sailing it more enjoyable.

- The association organises and publishes a large racing calendar annually. This covers local club races, national and international events for youths, seniors and masters (over 35).

- Some international associations offer coaching and training courses at a variety of levels, travel grants and special insurance discounts.

- The association will help put you in touch with a local club which races Lasers. Joining in club racing is the best way to improve your sailing. You will also meet fellow enthusiasts and probably become addicted to racing!

When you have mastered the skills in this book you should be able to win a club championship. If you would like to go further, *Laser Racing* by Ed Baird and *Championship Laser Racing* by Glenn Bourke, also published by Fernhurst Books, will help take you to World Championship standard.

   Good sailing!